Jungle Animals

Series Editor Deborah Lock
US Senior Editor Shannon Beatty
Editor Arpita Nath
Senior Art Editor Ann Cannings
Art Editor Yamini Panwar
Senior Producer, Pre-production Nikoleta Parasaki
Picture Researcher Sakshi Saluja
Jacket Designer Charlotte Jennings
DTP Designers Ashok Kumar and Dheeraj Singh
Managing Editor Soma B. Chowdhury
Managing Art Editor Ahlawat Gunjan
Art Director Martin Wilson

Reading Consultant
Linda Gambrell, Ph.D.

First American Edition, 2016
Published in the United States by DK Publishing
345 Hudson Street, New York, New York 10014

16 17 18 19 20 10 9 8 7 6 5 4 3
003—285392—June/16

Copyright © 2016 Dorling Kindersley Limited
All rights reserved. Without limiting the rights under copyright reserved above, no part of this publication may be reproduced, stored in or introduced into a retrieval system, or transmitted, in any form, or by any means (electronic, mechanical, photocopying, recording, or otherwise), without the prior written permission of the copyright owner. Published in Great Britain by Dorling Kindersley Limited.

A catalog record for this book is available
from the Library of Congress.

ISBN: 978-1-4654-4962-7 (Paperback)
ISBN: 978-1-4654-4963-4 (Hardback)

DK books are available at special discounts when purchased in bulk for sales promotions, premiums, fund-raising, or educational use. For details, contact:
DK Publishing Special Markets
345 Hudson Street, New York, New York 10014
SpecialSales@dk.com

Printed and bound in China.

The publisher would like to thank the following for their kind permission to reproduce their photographs:
(Key: a=above, b=below/bottom, c=center, l=left, r=right, t=top)
1 Getty Images: Anup Shah. **4 Dorling Kindersley:** Whipsnade Zoo, Bedfordshire (cra). **5** Philip Dowell: (crb). **Dreamstime.com:** Eric Isselee (cl). **Science Photo Library:** John Mitchell (tc). **6 naturepl.com:** Jack Dykinga (bl). **6–7 Corbis:** Jim Zuckerman. **8–9 naturepl.com:** Roland Seitre. **10–11 Corbis:** DLILLC. **12–13 Corbis:** Kevin Kurek/dpa. **14-15 naturepl.com:** Pete Oxford. **16-17 Alamy Images:** Design Pics Inc. **18-19 Getty Images:** heatherwest. **19 Robert Harding Picture Library:** Frans Lanting (c). **20-21 Getty Images:** Clara Zamith. **22 Alamy Images:** Design Pics Inc (bl); Arco Images GmbH (cla). **Dreamstime.com:** Eric Isselee (clb); Rinus Baak (cl). **24 naturepl.com:** Jack Dykinga (bl) *Endpapers:* **Dorling Kindersley:** Frank Greenaway. **Jacket credits:** *Front:* **Getty:** Heather West (c), Andy Rouse (tc). **dk.com:** Jerry Young (cl). *Back:* **dk.com:** Dave King, Courtesy of Whipsnade Zoo, Bedfordshire (tl)

All other images © Dorling Kindersley
For further information see: www.dkimages.com

A WORLD OF IDEAS:
SEE ALL THERE IS TO KNOW

www.dk.com

Contents

- 4   Enter the Jungle
- 6   Parrots
- 8   Toucans
- 10 Orangutans
- 12 Sun Bears
- 14 Giant Anteaters
- 16 Tarantulas
- 18 Tigers
- 20 Jaguars
- 22 Glossary
- 23 Index
- 24 Note to Parents

Enter the jungle,
if you dare!
Look up! Look down!
Look out!

Parrots

A parrot flies over the jungle. Its feathers flash red, yellow, green, and blue.

feathers

Toucans

A toucan picks
a berry with
its large, long beak.

Orangutans

Orangutans swing from tree to tree. They move very quickly.

Sun Bears

Sun bears climb the trees.
Their long claws grip the branches.

claw

Giant Anteaters

snout

14

An anteater sniffs an ants' nest with its long snout.

ants' nest

Tarantulas

ground

A tarantula feels the ground shake with its hairy legs.

hairy legs

Tigers

A tiger hides
in the grass.
It watches and waits,
ready to leap.

Jaguars

A jaguar rests.
Ssh!
Quiet in the jungle,
please!

Glossary

Beak
hard, pointed bird's mouth

Claws
sharp, curved toe-points

Feathers
soft covering on bird's body

Snout
long, pointed nose and mouth used to smell and eat

Spider's legs
hairy body parts used to move and sense animals nearby

Index

beak 8, 9

branch 13

claws 13

climb 13

feathers 6

giant anteaters 14–15

jaguars 20–21

orangutans 10

nest 15

parrots 6

snout 14, 15

sun bears 12–13

swing 10

tarantulas 16–17

tigers 18–19

toucans 8–9

A Note to Parents

DK Readers is a four-level interactive reading adventure series for children, designed in conjunction with leading literacy experts, including Dr. Linda Gambrell, Distinguished Professor of Education at Clemson University. Dr. Gambrell has served as President of the National Reading Conference, the College Reading Association, and the International Reading Association.

Beautiful illustrations and superb full-color photographs combine with engaging, easy-to-read stories to offer a fresh approach to each subject in the series. Each DK Reader is guaranteed to capture a child's interest while developing his or her reading skills, general knowledge, and love of reading.

The four levels of DK Readers are aimed at different reading abilities, enabling you to choose the books that are exactly right for your child:

Level 1: Learning to read
Level 2: Beginning to read
Level 3: Beginning to read alone
Level 4: Reading alone

The "normal" age at which a child begins to read can be anywhere from three to eight years old. Adult participation through the lower levels is very helpful for providing encouragement, discussing storylines, and sounding out unfamiliar words.

No matter which level you select, you can be sure that you are helping your child learn to read, then read to learn!